Fleshing out the Narrative

ALSO BY MARIËLLE S. SMITH

52 Weeks of Writing Author Journal and Planner, Vol. I: Get out of your own way and become the writer you're meant to be

52 Weeks of Writing Author Journal and Planner, Vol. II: Get out of your own way and become the writer you're meant to be

52 Weeks of Writing Author Journal and Planner, Vol. III: Get out of your own way and become the writer you're meant to be

365 Days of Gratitude Journal: Commit to the life-changing power of gratitude by creating a sustainable practice

365 Days of Gratitude Journal, Vol. II: Commit to the life-changing power of gratitude by creating a sustainable practice

Get Out of Your Own Way: A 31-Day Tarot Challenge for Writers and Other Creatives

Set Yourself Up for Success: A 31-Day Tarot Challenge for Writers and Other Creatives

Seven Simple Spreads 1: Seven Simple Card Spreads to Unlock Your Creative Flow

Seven Simple Spreads 2: Seven Simple Card Spreads to Direct Your Creative Flow

Seven Simple Spreads 3: Seven Simple Card Spreads to Boost Your Confidence

Seven Simple Spreads 4: Seven Simple Card Spreads to Celebrate Your Creative Wins

Speak Your Truth: A 31-Day Tarot Challenge for Writers and Other Creatives

Step into Your Power: A 31-Day Tarot Challenge to Unleash Your Creative Potential

Tarot for Creatives: 21 tarot spreads to (re)connect to your intuition and ignite that creative spark

CO-WRITTEN UNDER THE PEN NAME HEATHER MACLEE

Too Good to Be True?

Where There's a Will

There's a Way

FLESHING OUT THE NARRATIVE

A 31-day tarot and journal challenge for writers

Mariëlle S. Smith

Copyright © 2019 by M.S. Wordsmith

All rights reserved.

No part of this book may be reproduced in any form or by any electronic or mechanical means, including information storage and retrieval systems, without written consent of the copyright holder, except for the use of brief quotations in a book review.

ISBN 978 94 93250 03 1

Writing is wretched, discouraging, physically unhealthy, infinitely frustrating work. And when it all comes together it's utterly glorious.

Ralph Peters

Introduction

Welcome to *Fleshing Out the Narrative: A 31-Day Tarot and Journal Challenge for Writers*. Initially designed to help writers prepare for National Novel Writing Month (NaNoWriMo) in November, this challenge serves as a tool to help you uncover the hidden layers of your story and connect unforeseen dots.

Because *Fleshing Out the Narrative* was designed as a month-long challenge with one question per day, it does not cover each and every aspect of storytelling. Nevertheless, the questions presented to you during this challenge will still help you unravel what are considered the most important aspects of each and every story, namely the:

- premise
- theme
- hook
- setting
- main character
- antagonist
- confidant(e)
- foil, and
- mentor

Together, these aspects will go a long way in deepening your outline and preparing you for your first draft. Or deepen your next draft, in case you use the challenge to learn more about and add layers to a work already in progress.

Doing a tarot* challenge

So, how does a tarot challenge work? Quite simply, actually. Each day, you pick up your deck of choice, shuffle to your heart's content, and pick a card (or more, depending on the question and what your gut tells you). The next day, you put the card(s) back into your deck, shuffle like you mean it, and pull out your next draw.

To me, it doesn't matter how you shuffle your cards or decide which card is the one that needs picking. Just go with what you've been taught or what your gut tells you to do. There's really no doing this wrong.

The same goes with how you interpret the cards' messages. Some feel utterly comfortable using the guidebook that came with their deck, while others rely solely on their intuition. You can do either or a bit of both: when doing a reading, I don't mind glancing at the description offered by the creator of the cards, especially when I feel there is more to a card but I just can't seem to grasp the full meaning of it at the time. The guidebook won't always bridge that gap, but it might just give you another perspective, that 'Aha, of course!' moment that will kickstart your intuition. Whatever you do, don't let others tell you what is right and wrong: there's only a right and wrong for you, and you will know what is what in the moment.

I highly suggest that you write down your findings and reflect on them as you go. The same card might show up again and again: what could that mean? Some cards will only make sense later, after you answer a few more questions. Reflecting on previous draws will be especially relevant in those cases. And, even if all the cards make perfect sense the moment you draw them, looking at the bigger picture might still reveal something you had not considered before. It's in the reflecting that the wisdom lies.

*Use whatever works for you

Those familiar with my work know I don't differentiate between means of divination. I might use the word tarot, but you can use any deck of cards, whether that be tarot, oracle, or angel. If you'd rather use your crystals or your runes, feel free to go with that.

For those who want to do the challenge but aren't comfortable using either of those divinatory tools, or simply don't own any, I have turned each question into a journal exercise. I know of people who bought my first book and did just that without needing a separate prompt, but I have also had the question whether journaling would work as well more than once. Yes, it would and it does.

Likewise, if you would like to mix things up—perhaps the one question makes you want to grab your favourite oracle deck, while another makes you pick up a notebook—please do. Your challenge, your rules. As long as you follow your gut.

DAY 1

TAROT

What do I need to keep in mind about my story this month?

JOURNALING

Take a few deep breaths and settle into your writing space for today. Open your laptop or grab your favourite notebook and pen. Set your timer to fifteen minutes and ask yourself the following question:

What do I need to keep in mind about my story this month?

Don't think about it, just write.

THE PREMISE

The premise is the underlying idea of a story, the fundamental concept or foundation that supports the plot and drives the characters.

Every story has one premise, which can usually be summed up in a single sentence.

Day 2

Tarot

What do I need to know about my story's premise?

Journaling

Take a few deep breaths and settle into your writing space for today. Open your laptop or grab your favourite notebook and pen. Set your timer to fifteen minutes and ask yourself the following question:

What do I need to know about my story's premise?

Don't think about it, just write.

Day 3

Tarot

How does the story's premise serve the story as a whole?

Journaling

Take a few deep breaths and settle into your writing space for today. Open your laptop or grab your favourite notebook and pen. Set your timer to fifteen minutes and ask yourself the following question:

How does the story's premise serve the story as a whole?

Don't think about it, just write.

Day 4

Tarot

What about the premise needs to be fleshed out (more)?

Journaling

Take a few deep breaths and settle into your writing space for today. Open your laptop or grab your favourite notebook and pen. Set your timer to fifteen minutes and ask yourself the following question:

What about the premise needs to be fleshed out (more)?

Don't think about it, just write.

THE THEME

The theme is the deeper meaning or underlying message of a story, which can often be summed up in one or a few words.

A story tends to have multiple themes.

DAY 5

TAROT

What do I need to know about my story's theme(s)?

JOURNALING

Take a few deep breaths and settle into your writing space for today. Open your laptop or grab your favourite notebook and pen. Set your timer to fifteen minutes and ask yourself the following question:

What do I need to know about my story's theme(s)?

Don't think about it, just write.

Day 6

Tarot

How can I best apply my story's theme(s)?

Journaling

Take a few deep breaths and settle into your writing space for today. Open your laptop or grab your favourite notebook and pen. Set your timer to fifteen minutes and ask yourself the following question:

How can I best apply my story's theme(s)?

Don't think about it, just write.

Day 7

Tarot

What about my story's theme(s) needs to be fleshed out (more)?

Journaling

Take a few deep breaths and settle into your writing space for today. Open your laptop or grab your favourite notebook and pen. Set your timer to fifteen minutes and ask yourself the following question:

What about my story's theme(s) needs to be fleshed out (more)?

Don't think about it, just write.

The Hook

The hook is the opening of your story, and is meant to draw your reader straight in.

Preferably, the hook is just the opening sentence, but it could be the first few paragraphs or even pages.

DAY 8

TAROT

What do I need to know about my story's hook?

JOURNALING

Take a few deep breaths and settle into your writing space for today. Open your laptop or grab your favourite notebook and pen. Set your timer to fifteen minutes and ask yourself the following question:

What do I need to know about my story's hook?

Don't think about it, just write.

Day 9

Tarot

How does the hook serve the story as a whole?

Journaling

Take a few deep breaths and settle into your writing space for today. Open your laptop or grab your favourite notebook and pen. Set your timer to fifteen minutes and ask yourself the following question:

How does the hook serve the story as a whole?

Don't think about it, just write.

DAY 10

TAROT

What about the hook needs to be fleshed out (more)?

JOURNALING

Take a few deep breaths and settle into your writing space for today. Open your laptop or grab your favourite notebook and pen. Set your timer to fifteen minutes and ask yourself the following question:

What about the hook needs to be fleshed out (more)?

Don't think about it, just write.

THE SETTING

The setting is the ~~world~~ *word* in which your story takes place. This includes, but is not limited to, time, place, politics, social status, and period.

Settings can be real(istic) or (partly) made-up.

Day 11

Tarot

What do I need to know about my story's setting?

Journaling

Take a few deep breaths and settle into your writing space for today. Open your laptop or grab your favourite notebook and pen. Set your timer to fifteen minutes and ask yourself the following question:

What do I need to know about my story's setting?

Don't think about it, just write.

DAY 12

TAROT

What aspect(s) of my story's setting need(s) to be fleshed out (more)?

JOURNALING

Take a few deep breaths and settle into your writing space for today. Open your laptop or grab your favourite notebook and pen. Set your timer to fifteen minutes and ask yourself the following question:

What aspect(s) of my story's setting need(s) to be fleshed out (more)?

Don't think about it, just write.

Day 13

Tarot

How can my story's setting best aid / get in the way of the main character?
(Draw a card for each.)

Journaling

Take a few deep breaths and settle into your writing space for today. Open your laptop or grab your favourite notebook and pen. Set your timer to fifteen minutes and ask yourself the following question:

How can my story's setting best aid / get in the way of the main character?

Don't think about it, just write.

The Main Character

The main character is the most important character in a story. Stories can have multiple main characters.

The main character is also called the protagonist.

DAY 14

TAROT

What do I need to know about my story's main character?
(If your story has more than one main character, draw a card for each.)

JOURNALING

Take a few deep breaths and settle into your writing space for today. Open your laptop or grab your favourite notebook and pen. Set your timer to fifteen minutes and ask yourself the following question:

What do I need to know about my story's main character(s)?

Don't think about it, just write.

Day 15

Tarot

What do I need to know about the main character's flaw(s) / strength(s)?
(Draw a card for each.)

Journaling

Take a few deep breaths and settle into your writing space for today. Open your laptop or grab your favourite notebook and pen. Set your timer to fifteen minutes and ask yourself the following question:

What do I need to know about the main character's flaw(s) / strength(s)?

Don't think about it, just write.

Day 16

Tarot

How can the main character's flaw(s) / strength(s) best affect their character arc? (Draw a card for each.)

Journaling

Take a few deep breaths and settle into your writing space for today. Open your laptop or grab your favourite notebook and pen. Set your timer to fifteen minutes and ask yourself the following question:

How can the main character's flaw(s) / strength(s) best affect their character arc?

Don't think about it, just write.

Day 17

Tarot

How can the main character's flaw(s) / strength(s) best affect the story arc as a whole? (Draw a card for each.)

Journaling

Take a few deep breaths and settle into your writing space for today. Open your laptop or grab your favourite notebook and pen. Set your timer to fifteen minutes and ask yourself the following question:

How can the main character's flaw(s) / strength(s) best affect the story arc as a whole?

Don't think about it, just write.

The Antagonist

The antagonist is any force that forms an obstacle or has a goal that is in conflict with the main character's goal.

The antagonist can be anything from a (group of) character(s) to the main character's natural surroundings or some internal aspect.

DAY 18

TAROT

What do I need to know about my story's antagonist?

JOURNALING

Take a few deep breaths and settle into your writing space for today. Open your laptop or grab your favourite notebook and pen. Set your timer to fifteen minutes and ask yourself the following question:

What do I need to know about my story's antagonist?

Don't think about it, just write.

Day 19

Tarot

*What do I need to know about the antagonist's flaw(s) / strength(s)?
(Draw a card for each.)*

Journaling

Take a few deep breaths and settle into your writing space for today. Open your laptop or grab your favourite notebook and pen. Set your timer to fifteen minutes and ask yourself the following question:

What do I need to know about the antagonist's flaw(s) / strength(s)?

Don't think about it, just write.

Day 20

Tarot

How can the antagonist's flaw(s) / strength(s) best affect the main character's arc?
(Draw a card for each.)

Journaling

Take a few deep breaths and settle into your writing space for today. Open your laptop or grab your favourite notebook and pen. Set your timer to fifteen minutes and ask yourself the following question:

How can the antagonist's flaw(s) / strength(s) best affect the main character's arc?

Don't think about it, just write.

DAY 21

TAROT

How can the antagonist's flaw(s) / strength(s) best affect the story arc as a whole?
(Draw a card for each.)

JOURNALING

Take a few deep breaths and settle into your writing space for today. Open your laptop or grab your favourite notebook and pen. Set your timer to fifteen minutes and ask yourself the following question:

How can the antagonist's flaw(s) / strength(s) best affect the story arc as a whole?

Don't think about it, just write.

The Confidant(e)

Because the confidant(e) is trusted by the main character, they are crucial in helping the writer reveal the main character's inner world.

The confidant(e) helps the main character achieve their goal.

Day 22

Tarot

What do I need to know about my story's confidant(e)?

Journaling

Take a few deep breaths and settle into your writing space for today. Open your laptop or grab your favourite notebook and pen. Set your timer to fifteen minutes and ask yourself the following question:

What do I need to know about my story's confidant(e)?

Don't think about it, just write.

Day 23

Tarot

*What (un)seen aspect(s) of the confidant(e) can best affect the main character's arc?
(Draw multiple cards if needed.)*

Journaling

Take a few deep breaths and settle into your writing space for today. Open your laptop or grab your favourite notebook and pen. Set your timer to fifteen minutes and ask yourself the following question:

What (un)seen aspect(s) of the confidant(e) can best affect the main character's arc?

Don't think about it, just write.

Day 24

Tarot

What (un)seen aspect(s) of the confidant(e) can best affect the story arc as a whole?
(Draw multiple cards if needed.)

Journaling

Take a few deep breaths and settle into your writing space for today. Open your laptop or grab your favourite notebook and pen. Set your timer to fifteen minutes and ask yourself the following question:

What (un)seen aspect(s) of the confidant(e) can best affect the story arc as a whole?

Don't think about it, just write.

THE FOIL

(handwritten: Fool, of ils (oils))

The foil functions as a mirror in that their characteristics oppose those of the main character, either completely or through one key difference. This highlights certain traits of the main character.

The foil can be the antagonist or be someone who has the same goal as the main character.

DAY 25

TAROT

What do I need to know about my story's foil?

JOURNALING

Take a few deep breaths and settle into your writing space for today. Open your laptop or grab your favourite notebook and pen. Set your timer to fifteen minutes and ask yourself the following question:

What do I need to know about my story's foil?

Don't think about it, just write.

Day 26

Tarot

What (un)seen aspect(s) of the foil can best affect the main character's arc?
(Draw multiple cards if needed.)

Journaling

Take a few deep breaths and settle into your writing space for today. Open your laptop or grab your favourite notebook and pen. Set your timer to fifteen minutes and ask yourself the following question:

What (un)seen aspect(s) of the foil can best affect the main character's arc?

Don't think about it, just write.

DAY 27

TAROT

What (un)seen aspect(s) of the foil can best affect the story arc?
(Draw multiple cards if needed.)

JOURNALING

Take a few deep breaths and settle into your writing space for today. Open your laptop or grab your favourite notebook and pen. Set your timer to fifteen minutes and ask yourself the following question:

What (un)seen aspect(s) of the foil can best affect the story arc?

Don't think about it, just write.

Rome No Rent men
Net Ton OR rot
Note Rem Torn Tu
more more Tenor NOT
Tenor Note EON Rute
rote Tune No
rot Term me
Ten one

THE MENTOR

The mentor helps the main character in their quest, often by teaching them how they can help themselves.

The mentor tends to be older, and is generally regarded as a wise figure.

DAY 28

TAROT

What do I need to know about my story's mentor?

JOURNALING

Take a few deep breaths and settle into your writing space for today. Open your laptop or grab your favourite notebook and pen. Set your timer to fifteen minutes and ask yourself the following question:

What do I need to know about my story's mentor?

Don't think about it, just write.

Day 29

Tarot

What (un)seen aspect(s) of the mentor can best affect the main character's arc?
(Draw multiple cards if needed.)

Journaling

Take a few deep breaths and settle into your writing space for today. Open your laptop or grab your favourite notebook and pen. Set your timer to fifteen minutes and ask yourself the following question:

What (un)seen aspect(s) of the mentor can best affect the main character's arc?

Don't think about it, just write.

Day 30

Tarot

What (un)seen aspect(s) of the mentor can best affect the story arc as a whole?
(Draw multiple cards if needed.)

Journaling

Take a few deep breaths and settle into your writing space for today. Open your laptop or grab your favourite notebook and pen. Set your timer to fifteen minutes and ask yourself the following question:

What (un)seen aspect(s) of the mentor can best affect the story arc as a whole?

Don't think about it, just write.

Day 31

Tarot

Is there anything left I need to consider before I start writing?

Journaling

Take a few deep breaths and settle into your writing space for today. Open your laptop or grab your favourite notebook and pen. Set your timer to fifteen minutes and ask yourself the following question:

Is there anything left I need to consider before I start writing?

Don't think about it, just write.

Please consider leaving a review

Authors are nowhere without honest reviews, and I'd truly appreciate it if you left one on Goodreads, my Facebook page facebook.com/mswordsmith, or the retailer where you bought this book.

The Creative Cardslingers

Isn't it better to sling cards together?

Join my private Facebook group The Creative Cardslingers (password **AQUAMARINE**) to meet fellow creative cardreaders, be the first to test my latest card spreads, and hear all about the creative projects I'm involved in.

Want More?

Head over to mswordsmith.nl/starterkit and get my free Get Out of Your Own Way Starter Kit now.

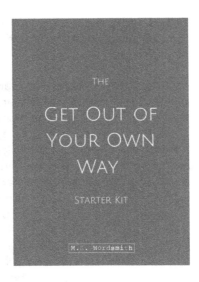

The Get Out of Your Own Way Starter Kit includes four different tools:

- An exercise on limiting beliefs,
- a monthly tracking and reflecting worksheet,
- a meditation on letting go of limiting beliefs,
- a tarot spread on creative roadblocks (from *Tarot for Creatives*),

and is yours when signing up to my newsletter.

About Me

I'm a coach for writers and other creatives, an editor, a writer, an intuitive healer, and a custom retreat organiser. Born in the Netherlands and raised by my Dutch mother and Scottish expat father, I moved to the island of Cyprus in February 2019.

The thing about being somewhere new is that it sheds a different light on your life. Your mind opens up to other perspectives, and you find yourself brimming with new ideas. Or old ideas you never wanted to take seriously suddenly demand your attention.

Bringing the spiritual into my work was a scary step for me, because I've always tried to keep the two separate. I say 'tried' because quite a few of my clients, and the work they brought with them, have forced me to merge my professional background with my spiritual interests. Some hired me to edit or translate their holistic books, others came to me for coaching and were struggling in a way that needed a broader approach. And then there are the many writers and other creatives who are openly incorporating spirituality into their practice as we speak.

Over the past year, I've switched gears and gradually allowed the spiritual to enter my workspace. This book is one of its many manifestations. It goes without saying that I hope you'll enjoy it, and get from it everything you need.

Want to get in touch? There are different ways and places to contact me:

Website: mswordsmith.nl
E-mail: marielle@mswordsmith.nl
instagram.com/mariellessmith
facebook.com/mswordsmith